# THE CONCISE
# LESSONS
# IN
# CHEMISTRY

A NOVEL

BONNIE GARMUS

@Copyright 2023

All rights reserved @Copyright 2023.

Without the express written consent of the author and/or publisher, no portion of this book may be copied, reproduced, or transmitted in any form.

Neither the publisher nor the author will be held directly or indirectly liable for any damages, reparation, or financial loss caused by the information included in this book.

## LEGAL NOTICE:

This book has copy protections in place. This is for your own private use only. Nothing in this book may be copied, reproduced, transmitted, displayed, used, quoted, or paraphrased in any form without the prior written permission of the author and/or publisher.

## DISCLAIMER NOTICE:

The contents of this paper are intended solely for your own growth and enjoyment. Information presented is current, correct, reliable, and comprehensive to the best of our ability. There are no express or implied guarantees of any sort. The reader understands that no professional, legal, financial, or medical advice is being given. The information contained in this book comes from a wide range of original resources. Before attempting any of the methods described here, you should get the advice of a qualified expert.

The reader accepts that the author will not be held liable for any damages (whether monetary or otherwise) resulting from the use of the information provided herein, regardless of whether such material turns out to be free of mistakes, omissions, or inaccuracies.

ISBN: 978-1-312-15501-5

Cover Design by Bensmiles

Published by FCOACHES

Written by Benson Stephen

## DISCLAIMER:

This synopsis should be viewed as something other than a replacement for the original work. Anyone interested in supporting the author, Bonnie Garmus, is strongly encouraged to read the actual book for the whole experience.

# Table of Contents

Legal Notice: ................................................................................................... 2

Disclaimer Notice: ........................................................................................... 2

Disclaimer: ...................................................................................................... 3

Introduction .................................................................................................... 6

Chapter 1: November 1961 .............................................................................. 7

Chapter 2: Pine ................................................................................................ 8

Chapter 3: Hastings Institution for Research ................................................... 9

Chapter 4: Introduction to Chemistry ............................................................ 11

Chapter 5: Values in the Family ..................................................................... 12

Part 6: The Hastings Cafeteria ....................................................................... 14

Chapter 7: Six-Thirty ...................................................................................... 15

Chapter 8: Overreaching ................................................................................ 16

Chapter 9: The Grudge ................................................................................... 18

Chapter 10: The Leash ................................................................................... 19

Chapter 11: Budget Cuts ................................................................................ 20

Chapter 12: Calvin's Parting Gift .................................................................... 21

Chapter 13: Idiots .......................................................................................... 23

Chapter 14: Grief ........................................................................................... 24

Chapter 15: Unsolicited Advice ...................................................................... 25

Chapter 16: Labor .......................................................................................... 26

Chapter 17: The Harriet Sloane ...................................................................... 27

Chapter 18: Legally Mad ................................................................................ 29

Chapter 19: December 1956 .......................................................................... 30

Chapter 20: Life Story .................................................................................... 31

Chapter 21: E.Z. ............................................................................................. 32

Chapter 22: The Present ................................................................................ 33

Chapter 23: KCTV Studios .............................................................................. 34

Chapter 24: The Afternoon Zone of Depression ............................................................. 36

Chapter 25: The Average Jane ........................................................................................ 38

Chapter 26: The Funeral ................................................................................................. 39

Chapter 27: All About Me ............................................................................................... 40

Chapter 28: Saints .......................................................................................................... 42

Chapter 29: Bonding ...................................................................................................... 44

Chapter 30: 99 Percent .................................................................................................. 46

Chapter 31: The Get-Well Card ..................................................................................... 48

Chapter 32: Medium Rare ............................................................................................. 49

Chapter 33: Faith ........................................................................................................... 50

Chapter 34: All Saints .................................................................................................... 51

Chapter 35: The Smell of Failure ................................................................................... 52

Chapter 36: Life and Death ........................................................................................... 53

Chapter 37: Sold Out ..................................................................................................... 54

Chapter 38: Brownies .................................................................................................... 55

Chapter 39: Dear Sirs .................................................................................................... 56

Chapter 40: Normal ....................................................................................................... 57

Chapter 41: Recommit ................................................................................................... 58

Chapter 42: Personnel ................................................................................................... 59

Chapter 43: Stillborn ..................................................................................................... 60

Chapter 44: The Acorn .................................................................................................. 61

Chapter 45: Supper at Six ............................................................................................. 62

Dear Reader ................................................................................................................... 63

# INTRODUCTION

This Concise has been meticulously crafted with helpful additions and page references to help readers get the most out of the No. 1 Global Bestseller.

Elizabeth Zott is a brilliant and severely underappreciated scientist in the 1960s male-dominated scientific community. After being unjustly sacked, she is reluctant to host the cooking show Supper at Six, aimed at the typical housewife. Her goal isn't to make her female audience feel comfortable around science and chemistry; she happens to be smiling and making cocktails while doing it.

Her adventure begins when she meets Calvin Evans, her chemical and romantic counterpart. When their love story is cut short, Elizabeth and their intelligent dog, Six-thirty, are left to pick up the pieces as they navigate the challenges of scientific research, relationships, bothersome coworkers, and rowing.

But there are questions about her significant other's dark history that not even the bright Elizabeth knows. She had no idea that yet another of his surprises for her is on its way.

She finds herself at a loss after being fired from the one profession she had ever taken pride in. That is until she meets Walter, a frantic producer under pressure to cast a TV star before the show's premiere. Her play, Supper at Six, is top-rated among the general public, but it has also angered the more traditional members of society and the show's executive producer.

Her entire life, including her pioneering chemical research, she was constantly talked over and ignored, but she managed to come out on top. This time, though, she will need more than willpower to pull herself out of a deep melancholy.

With the support of her newfound family—her neighbor Walter, a coxswain, a dog who can read, and a minister—she must summon the will to face each day with the determination to prove her skeptics wrong through rigorous scientific analysis.

## CHAPTER 1: NOVEMBER 1961

Elizabeth Zott, Madeline's no-nonsense thirty-year-old mother, was preparing a lunch for her daughter, five-year-old Madeline. The two of them had a home in Commons, a town in Southern California that was just as boring as its name suggested.

Elizabeth, who was clinically depressed, made it a habit to provide notes for her daughter's lunches every day in which she advised her on how to blend in without standing out too much. On that note, she advised against giving the boys too much of an advantage in sports and stated her belief that nearly everyone is terrible.

Madeline was so much smarter than her peers that she could easily decipher these notes, but she never let on about her superior reading skills in class. She had no illusions that her classmates wouldn't eventually catch up to her reading level and that her gift would do anything but annoy them.

Elizabeth, the host of the food show Supper at Six, is clearly troubled by something from her past as she drives to work.

It's an unusually brief introduction at just two pages long, yet it answers the essential question: "What happened to the mysterious Elizabeth Zott?"

## CHAPTER 2: PINE

*New characters*

- Calvin Evans: someone linked to Elizabeth's past
- Walter Pine: Amanda's TV producer father
- Amanda Pine: the girl stealing Madeline's lunch

It's clear that Madeline felt out of place at school due to her gifts, so she attempted to bribe her way into Amanda Pine's good graces. What is it? Madeline's parents made her a special lunch to give her all the nutrients she needed as a young girl. Elizabeth's calls to Amanda's father, Walter Pine, were answered when she discovered Madeline's remarkable weight loss, at which point she decided to face him at his employment.

Elizabeth's frankness and beauty shocked the TV show's producer. Despite his assumption that she was interviewing for a nursing position, she spoke to him like a supervisor and lectured him on the significance of his daughter eating independently.

Previously, Elizabeth worked as a chemist at the Hastings Research Institute, but following her presentation to Mr. Pine, she was offered a new position. Supper at Six began because she had proposed the idea of training people across the country to cook with intention. Because of the humiliation she felt for being a woman in the field of chemistry, she quickly abandoned it in favor of the higher-paying TV program.

Her vast, healthy meals and no-nonsense approach to cooking made her popular among fans and earned her the derogatory moniker "Luscious Lizzie." This meant that her actual name couldn't take credit for her success. But things weren't what they seemed, and readers will recall that a new figure, Calvin Evans, played a role in the beginning of Elizabeth's troubles.

In this chapter, we learn that Madeline's intellect makes it hard for her to make friends and that Elizabeth's depression is tied to Calvin Evans; these themes will be developed more in the following chapter.

# CHAPTER 3: HASTINGS INSTITUTION FOR RESEARCH

*Updated and redesigned characters*

- Calvin Evans: a famous chemist and rower
- Dr. Donatti: Elizabeth and Calvin's boss at Hastings
- Dr. Meyers: Elizabeth's ex-thesis-advisor at the University of California

Ten years ago, reclusive genius, grudge holder, and rower Calvin Evans settled on Commons as his place of employment over numerous other offers centered in wetter climates.

He had already proven himself a prodigy by the time he was a teenager, and he was now pursuing his interest in chemistry at the Hastings Research Institute, where Elizabeth also worked.

His own spacious laboratory had been set aside for him, while his less famous and female colleagues had to make do with less room and fewer resources. Elizabeth, taking the initiative, walked into his lab despite the numerous no-entry signs in order to steal some beakers she required for her investigation.

Their initial encounter was tense because Calvin mistook her for a secretary, prompting her to steal his beakers. The next time they saw each other, Calvin made an attempt to ask her out, but she was uninterested and he had no dating experience.

When word got around that she had spoken ill of the famous chemist behind her back, her coworkers were outraged. As a PhD student at the University of California, Berkeley, Elizabeth experienced trauma that was caused by a single word.

She remembered the traumatic event as a late night encounter with her thesis advisor, Dr. Meyers, during which she discovered an error on a test. She questioned him about it, but he dismissed her worries and continued to use the slur. He made a pass at sexually assaulting her, but she defended herself by stabbing him with a pencil. The police didn't buy her account, so she was expelled for making it up to clear Meyers' name.

She still keeps a pencil in her hair to this day because of this very reason.

Elizabeth is currently working on a new research topic unrelated to the one she was nearly finished with. Dr. Donatti, her boss, had been the one to use the trigger word, and his choice had been final.

After two weeks, Elizabeth and Calvin both happened to be at the theater on dates. Calvin threw up on Elizabeth after he and his stomach had a run-in over his displeasure with the performance. Elizabeth, however, seemed unfazed by this, and she guided him securely back to his house.

They reconnected, and Elizabeth revealed that she had been reassigned from her research on abiogenesis, the hypothesis that life arose from nonliving origins. Elizabeth said that sexism was to blame for the reallocation, but Calvin denied the existence of prejudice and couldn't fathom why any woman would want to pursue a career in science.

He proposed getting involved himself to make Donatti reconsider. Elizabeth was hesitant to grant this favor, but after Calvin advised her to use the system to her benefit rather than be a victim of it, she gave in. The two partners publicly committed to a professional alliance but privately yearned for more.

## CHAPTER 4: INTRODUCTION TO CHEMISTRY

After working together for weeks, Elizabeth and Calvin finally had a falling out in the parking lot. When Elizabeth used a silkworm analogy to convey the romantic sentiments she had acquired for Calvin, he meant that she no longer had any interest in him.

Elizabeth acted on her suppressed feelings when Calvin knocked on her car window shortly after they were separated, and she kissed him.

It was difficult for them to separate due to their mutual fascination and irritation. They fought because their values weren't aligned, but their attraction and love of chemistry made it obvious that they were meant to be together.

In subsequent chapters, we'll see both characters develop more, with Calvin shedding his naiveté and Elizabeth finally learning to accept help.

# CHAPTER 5: VALUES IN THE FAMILY

*Fresh faces*

- Calvin's Father: a mysterious character
- John Zott: Elizabeth's deceased brother

There were rumors that Elizabeth and Calvin were only dating because of her attractiveness or his celebrity, but the truth was that they were closer than ever.

After they had spent the night together, Calvin brought up the subject of family for the first time. Calvin disclosed that he had a challenging upbringing, losing his parents at age five in a train disaster and then his aunt at age six in a car accident.

Since it was now her chance to talk about her background, Elizabeth refrained from pressing the issue of how he managed to get to Cambridge after spending his childhood in an orphanage and learning to row.

Elizabeth's mother produced the props that her father, a religious con man, used to trick people out of their money. Elizabeth's interest in chemistry can be traced back to when he used pistachios to produce fire as a "convenient sign from God" (Garmus, 2022, p. 37) to help sell the scam.

Calvin, who had always desired a family of his own, couldn't fathom why she was at odds with hers. Elizabeth said that her father emotionally harassed and rejected her brother John because he was gay and that John took his own life when he was seventeen.

When her father passed away, she could not continue her formal education because her family frequently relocated. Her father is imprisoned for a failed tax fraud scheme, and her mother remarried in Brazil.

The young Calvin shared the encouraging mantra he used to tell himself: "Every day was new" (Garmus, 2022, p. 40). In subsequent chapters, this will become crucial information.

He was mid-sentence when a startling thought about his father cut him off. They agreed to continue discussing it tomorrow, but that was a lie.

Calvin's abandonment issues (which will recur later) and Elizabeth's great independence can be traced back to their respective histories. Both had forgotten the joys of childhood and were repressing their traumatic records.

The truth about Calvin's father, which he has been hiding from Elizabeth, will emerge soon.

# PART 6: THE HASTINGS CAFETERIA

*Fresh faces*

- Miss Frask: a secretary at Hastings

This chapter is written from the viewpoint of three geologists and Miss Frask, a secretary who works with Elizabeth and Calvin in the cafeteria. Miss Frask is dating a geologist named Eddie, and the rest of the gang is envious of the happy couple.

Calvin's third candidacy for the Nobel Peace Prize was laughed at, as was Elizabeth's home-cooked lunch and then Calvin's engagement ring.

Although it was frowned upon, Elizabeth and her boyfriend were living together; she was expected to contribute to the couple's shared expenses by providing a home-cooked meal since her wage wasn't enough. Calvin used Elizabeth's comment about becoming a substitute bridesmaid in a friend's wedding as an excuse to pop the question.

But Elizabeth had already made it known that she would never get married. She was worried that she would lose her individuality if they were married because her successes would be associated with Calvin's surname. And because her thrice-remarried misogynistic mother believed that no woman could refuse marriage, she swore off marriage altogether.

Calvin, who should have known better, dismissed the idea of adopting her last name out of concern for his reputation. Though he no longer desired to marry her, he brought up the concept of starting a family again, which Elizabeth mistook for suggesting they form a family through procreation. To the dismay of the group rooting for their breakup, Elizabeth gladly accepted his puppy offer.

This chapter reinforced Elizabeth's ideas on marriage and motherhood, which she equated with a woman's subjugation and reliance. She wanted to be recognized for her efforts rather than her spouse's, but Calvin pointed out in Chapter 3 that this was extremely unlikely for a woman in their day. She regarded his advice to leverage his contacts and her studies as dependent on him.

It would mean a lot if you took a few minutes out of your day to leave a review or rating on the site you purchased the book from if you are enjoying it so far. Did you realize that only about 0.5 - 1 % of readers write a testimonial? Much obliged:)

## CHAPTER 7: SIX-THIRTY

*New characters*

- Six-Thirty: Elizabeth and Calvin's found ex-bomb-sniffer dog
- The coxswain, Dr. Mason: commander of the boat of rowers and an obstetrician, a medical professional focused on pregnancy and childbirth

When Calvin asked Elizabeth who the dog was, she mistook the time and said 6:30 p.m., and the dog eventually became a member of the family. Being a former bomb-sniffer dog made him exceptionally bright and quick to learn new orders. Unlike the less complex German Shepherds, Sixthirty couldn't bring himself to seek out and martyr himself on the lethal explosives. As a result, he felt completely alone and developed a severe aversion to noise.

Six-thirty is portrayed in an anthropomorphic manner, which means he is endowed with human traits such as independent cognition, which are disclosed gradually to the reader.

Now that he had his dream family, Calvin couldn't wait to get Elizabeth involved in rowing. Calvin insinuated that Elizabeth's lack of enthusiasm stemmed from her belief that "women can't row" (Garmus, 2022, p.62).

To show him he was wrong, she accompanied Calvin to a boathouse, where he began training on an erg, an indoor rowing machine. The coxswain and eight rowers walked in, and Calvin stood in their path. His hyperfocus was induced by the coxswain's yelling of orders and rough motivation. Despite feeling emotionally and physically drained, Calvin had introduced Elizabeth as his new rowing partner.

Knowing that she would forever be associated with Calvin Evans as a rowing partner made it impossible for Elizabeth to back out.

Elizabeth had been pushed out of her comfort zone with the aid of Calvin. Rowing became a major part of her life as she worked hard to prove that women should be treated equally and can achieve everything they set their minds to.

## CHAPTER 8: OVERREACHING

*New characters*

- The wealthy sponsor: mysteriously funds Hastings with the sole interest of abiogenesis.
- Dr. Boryweitz: Elizabeth's anxious colleague

Training in the pair (a two-person boat) for several days yielded no results. Calvin believed that, as a novice and a woman, she would never be allowed into the all-male group, even if the eight-seater boat was said to be simpler to row. Despite her inability to swim, Elizabeth made tremendous progress after she reduced her comprehension of rowing to scientific calculations.

Although she improved as a rower, her research fell by the wayside when Donatti told her she wasn't smart enough to continue.

The next section of the chapter is told from Donatti's point of view, and it shows how much he despises Calvin, how jealous he is, and how sexist he is. He plots revenge against Calvin by falling for Elizabeth, and he begins by criticizing her intelligence to destroy her self-esteem.

Elizabeth shared her disappointment with Dr. Boryweitz, another dissatisfied lab worker after Donatti once again denied her research.

Even after several weeks, she abandoned the project, and Calvin couldn't help but get involved behind her back. Calvin made the threat of leaving and taking his fame and investor money with him. If not for the appearance of a mysterious major league sponsor who was exclusively interested in abiogenesis (Elizabeth's research topic), Donatti would have been happy with this.

Elizabeth was overjoyed that she had finally succeeded in having her research project funded.

After that, Calvin tried to get back in the action by lobbying the coxswain to let Elizabeth row in the eight-seater. Dr. Mason, the coxswain, was an obstetrician who knew the strength of women but was still skeptical until Calvin offered to row with them as a negotiating point.

Calvin cited her impressive rowing as an excuse for Elizabeth's unexpected acceptance. Even if she hadn't told him, he still would have known she couldn't swim, so he got her a seat in the back of the eight-seater boat.

Calvin blamed himself for the deaths of everyone he cared about, and considered himself a source of misfortune. His fear of losing Elizabeth made him try to shield her from harm even though he knew her distaste for such measures. His obsessiveness and overprotection may derive from his inability to bear the thought of losing another loved one, brought on by his abandonment issues.

In the car, Elizabeth brought up how she had never witnessed Calvin's reputation for carrying grudges. He claimed he had no lingering resentment toward anyone. As we move on to the following chapter, you'll see how ironic this remark is.

# CHAPTER 9: THE GRUDGE

*New characters*

- The wealthy man: a mystery and perhaps Calvin's biological father
- The Bishop; the Head of Staff at All Saints

In this chapter, we learn about the one thing that made Calvin bitter for the rest of his life and how it all started in a Catholic boys' orphanage called All Saints.

When Calvin was ten years old, a wealthy man unexpectedly visited the orphanage and left behind a large donation of educational resources like games, worksheets, and books. Later, after being chastised for telling the truth, Calvin discovered that books on evolution had been confiscated, presumably by the orphanage.

The bishop corrected Calvin's impression that he was an orphan by explaining that his biological parents had adopted him before their deaths five years prior. His father couldn't manage being a single dad, and he was informed his mother died in childbirth. The bishop suggested that the wealthy guy was Calvin's absent father, but the man showed no interest in kidnapping Calvin.

Calvin immersed himself in chemistry and physics because of his insatiable curiosity and his need to learn more about his mystery father.

Both Elizabeth and Calvin's early experiences with chemistry originated in sadness and grief, in Elizabeth's case over the loss of her brother and Calvin's case over the loss of his parents.

In this flashback, we can infer that the bishop's words rekindled Calvin's feelings of rejection and abandonment. The reader can sympathize with his worry about losing Elizabeth as an adult in light of his ongoing degradation and sense of rejection.

## CHAPTER 10: THE LEASH

*New characters*

- Calvin's ex-pen pal: a religious man who stopped writing back when Calvin mentioned his opinion of his father

In the present, after learning of the mandated use of leashes for canine companions, Elizabeth purchased one for Six-thirty. The sudden increase in animal fatalities caused by automobiles worried her greatly. She insisted that Calvin use the leash whenever he walked Six-thirty, but he opposed doing so because it would prevent him from jogging freely.

A rowing competition that Calvin indicated would take place the following week brought positive attention to the couple.

Given his celebrity, he recalled the letters he'd gotten from an "uncle," "brother," and "mother," all of whom claimed to be long-lost relatives in dire need of financial assistance. Even though he had never replied, the letter brought back fond memories of a long-lost penfriend. In Chapter 5, Calvin finally wrote about his evasive reaction to thinking about his father.

Instead of falling asleep, Elizabeth woke early and headed to the office. Calvin got up an hour later and, rather than drive himself and Elizabeth home, he decided to run to work with Six-thirty. He couldn't shake the fear that she would perish in a vehicle accident like his aunt had. He took the leash with him to respect Elizabeth's request.

The story finishes with the devastating note that Calvin had recently passed away.

## CHAPTER 11: BUDGET CUTS

Calvin and Six-thirty had run past the police station countless times during his murder. However, the police needed to have kept their vehicles in good working order due to budget shortages. They were startled by a loud noise from one of the poorly maintained vehicles. Six hundred thirty tugged on the leash in the opposite direction of Calvin, and while they wrestled, the dog ended up on the road after slipping on some motor oil. Early that morning, he was run over by a police car that didn't see him.

Six-thirty stood on the opposite side of the road from where Calvin had been flung, helplessly watching as he bled from the fall. Calvin's wrist and Six-thirty's collar still had the remaining pieces of the broken leash attached. Perhaps this is a metaphor for the end of their relationship, as Calvin died soon after.

The leash's presence raises intriguing possibilities about what might have happened if Calvin hadn't listened to Elizabeth or gone to work with her instead. Tragically, Calvin's death was tied to the very trait of less stubbornness that he was developing: accepting the leash.

The chain of circumstances that culminated in the tragedy can be seen as a manifestation of the butterfly effect. Elizabeth's worries about the leash rule, Calvin's use of it, and Six-thirty's frightened reaction due to his previous experience as a bomb sniffer, all stemmed from the decision to cut police budget.

## CHAPTER 12: CALVIN'S PARTING GIFT

*New characters*

- Reporter who swayed public opinion with their writing

Elizabeth was eight years old when her brother dared her to dive into a quarry full of water. She was not a good swimmer but tried nevertheless. Her brother rescued her then, but she wishes she hadn't been.

Elizabeth, who bought the leash on which Calvin choked to death, naturally felt guilty and responsible. She and Six-thirty went into profound despair but found the strength to give the mortician Six-thirty's rowing clothing for burial. They destroyed those garments and dressed him in a suit.

Even though they secretly celebrated because they were jealous of Calvin, many rowers and Hastings workers attended the funeral to express their condolences.

Six-thirty understood Elizabeth's depression, which presented itself in suicidal ideation. But the dog and the woman cared for each other so much that they were both willing to keep going.

They were standing quite a distance from the funeral, and a reporter saw this as an opportunity to grill her about her relationship with Calvin, his family, and his weaknesses. He mistook her lack of reaction and expression for blindness and guided her toward the crowd, only to be taken aback when she resisted. As he persisted in bringing up the rumor that Calvin was "a jerk" (Garmus, 202 2, p. 100), he assumed that her denial was due to her misinterpreting his words rather than the other way around.

Even though he hadn't yet learned that Elizabeth was Calvin's partner, his tone was arrogant and harsh as he made nasty comments about Calvin. The assumption that she is odd or needs his assistance just by being alive may indicate the casual misogyny of the time.

As Elizabeth and Sixty-three made their way home from the burial, they noticed the first signs of spring in the flowers they passed. Elizabeth's lowest point coinciding with Spring, a season often associated with renewal and hope, provides irony and may foreshadow change.

Being home without Calvin was too much to bear, so they went to work. Elizabeth's coworkers avoided her when they saw she was emotionally fragile. When she and Six-thirty went into Calvin's lab, they found all his belongings had been boxed up and were waiting to be picked up by a member of his immediate family. Elizabeth was prohibited from looking at or taking anything because she and Calvin were not married. Since this was an act of mercy on Calvin's part, Miss Frask, the office secretary from Chapter 6, notified her that Six-thirty was no longer welcome at work. Elizabeth had already removed the ring with which Calvin had proposed to her, unbeknownst to Frask.

Miss Frask indicated that Elizabeth rode his coattails, which means she took advantage of his success for her gain. She implied that Elizabeth and Calvin's relationship was meaningless and superficial.

Frask disliked Elizabeth because she was lovely and nonconformist; he advised that she give up chemistry in favor of having a large family. Just before Elizabeth threw up in the sink, she told her to take extra time off.

Frask presented Elizabeth with a newspaper story written by the reporter at the funeral. The piece implied that Calvin's unlikable personality hurt his work and that even his partner had little personal knowledge of him. Once again, Elizabeth vomited.

Elizabeth didn't know she was pregnant until Frask pointed it out after she threw up.

The chapter displayed a shocking lack of compassion, from Calvin's coworkers' celebration of his death to Frask's treatment of Elizabeth. As readers, we know the truth, but Elizabeth and Calvin's joy must have seemed undeserved to anyone looking in. They have the nerve to find happiness when everyone else is suffering.

This demonstrates that envy and greed are symptoms of a deeper problem: people's dislike of themselves and dissatisfaction with their lives. People in the '60s took out their discontent on others because they followed the status quo, prioritizing what society thought was right over their happiness.

This chapter is a prime example of the book's central theme: the disastrous results of rigid thinking and lack of knowledge.

## CHAPTER 13: IDIOTS

The chapter opens with a first-person account of Hastings Management's heartless corporate strategy of using all means required to acquire funds.

In a flash forward to Chapter 8, we learn that Calvin was persistent in pursuing adequate financing for abiogenesis, arguing that Elizabeth's "ideas might even be better than his own" (Garmus, 2022, p. 110).

Current events show that the negative impression of Calvin left by the news item impacted Hastings since investors questioned the company's financial backing. But at the last minute, a mysterious wealthy patron interested in abiogenesis materialized.

Hastings portrayed Elizabeth as a male and then made it such that the man financing her couldn't meet her. Hastings would be doomed if it were revealed that the chemist was a single pregnant lady. Miss Frask had also spread the news that Elizabeth was expecting.

Hastings had intended to replace her with one of the three other chemists she had been working with, but it turned out that she was the only capable one. Even Dr. Boryweitz tried to steal the spotlight, but he was exposed.

Elizabeth was to be fired as quickly as possible by Miss Frask and Dr. Donatti. They were taken aback when Elizabeth casually mentioned her pregnancy as a possible explanation. Women were usually blamed for these problems, while males carried on as usual. Elizabeth, a woman, offended Donatti by explaining pregnancy to him. Even though Elizabeth knew it wasn't authorized by company policy, he argued that the rationale was valid.

Donatti casually stated that Calvin insisted they back her project as they rushed her out. This development took Elizabeth aback. Her faith had been betrayed, and everything in her life was disintegrating.

## CHAPTER 14: GRIEF

A gravestone for Calvin was erected, but the inscribed phrase was lopped off, leaving just the words "Your days are numbered" (Garmus, 2022, p. 116) (see also: lack of forethought). In light of Calvin's unexpected death, Elizabeth's present outlook on life is mirrored in the statement's gloomy tone: time is precious, and life is brief.

Elizabeth was employing a standard method for teaching young children; she had Six-thirty Words look at pictures in books to help him learn the meanings of words through association.

Six-thirty utilized these terms to have mental conversations with others and to try to have a conversation with the baby growing inside of Elizabeth. The cemetery groundskeeper wouldn't let him visit Calvin's grave as he worried about Elizabeth's mental health during his frequent travels there. A few months ago, she demolished the kitchen in order to make a place for a laboratory in her house. She made do with what she had by using her skills in home improvement and repurposing. A very effective and cutting-edge laboratory was the result.

A large number of Hastings' chemists arrived after Elizabeth was let go, making it clear that they were at a loss without her. She saw an opportunity to make money, so she began charging clients for her services and doing their work in the same manner as her previous job.

The more Elizabeth overextended herself and ignored her health, the more worried Six-thirty became. The groundskeeper discovered Six-thirty during one conversation with Calvin and shot at him. Because of the injury he sustained, Six-Thirty was going to bite him but instead barked for assistance. When it came to compassion, Six-Thirty had a greater grasp on it than the average person.

Assuring Elizabeth that he would portray Six-thirty in a positive light, the news reporter from the funeral brought him back home safely. In doing so, he ultimately led to the dismissal of the groundskeeper.

A photograph of Calvin's tombstone taken by the groundskeeper appeared in the story, and Elizabeth recognized it immediately. New words have been added: "Your days are nu" (Garmus, 2022, p. 124), which can be pronounced "Your days are new." Similar to what was said in Chapter 5, this is a phrase that Calvin used to tell his younger self. It's possible that Calvin is using this coincidence to inspire Elizabeth from beyond the grave, just as he did in life. Every day is a fresh start, fraught with new difficulties and opportunities.

## CHAPTER 15: UNSOLICITED ADVICE

My everyday existence as a pregnant lady was fraught with unpleasant comments from strangers. Many people felt compelled to reassure Elizabeth that her current discomfort was just temporary, while others felt compelled to guess the gender of her unborn child.

In the wake of her altercation with the groundskeeper, Elizabeth had a new headstone erected for Calvin, this one bearing an intricate formula for the "chemical response" that produced "happiness" (Garmus, 2022, p. 127). They shared a secret understanding no one else shared, strengthening their love and relationship.

Elizabeth scheduled a checkup with the coxswain's doctor, Dr. Mason. A man tapped her stomach like a drum without her permission in the elevator on the way to the office, prompting her to reply with a pocketbook to the crotch.

Elizabeth's admission that she'd been erging caught Dr. Mason off guard. He acknowledged that it would help her get ready for birth, but he couldn't fathom why she would subject herself to such discomfort. She lied when he inquired why she came in so late and said she was busy at work.

Her overexertion while erging and the postponement of her first check-up were both cover stories for the truth that she secretly hoped she would lose the baby.

After completing his examination, Dr. Mason told her he understood her struggles. When someone finally understood her plight, she broke down in tears.

Mason carefully stated that he didn't pass judgment and could relate to her predicament. He believed that women shouldn't be forced to give birth to children against their will. When he asked if she had any help with the baby, she could only think about her dog.

Mason didn't appear surprised by her response and instead offered her a seat in his boat until she could return to rowing.

He was the first person since Calvin to treat her properly, without asking awkward questions or making assumptions about her because she was still unmarried to Calvin and preferred to be addressed as Miss Zott rather than Mrs. Evans. This kindness was her ray of sunshine, her fresh start, and she realized she wasn't crazy for feeling like she did.

# CHAPTER 16: LABOR

Several weeks later, Six-thirty's vocabulary had significantly expanded, and Elizabeth was on the verge of borrowing some new books for him. Elizabeth believed she was hungry as she walked to the library. She had tracked her cycle and thought she knew when she would give birth, but she was actually in labor.

After a grueling 13 hours of labor, Dr. Mason delivered a healthy baby girl and predicted that she would excel as a rower. Elizabeth checked out of recovery the following day with the pretext that she needed to erg, despite being pushed to stay for a few more days.

Six-thirty thought the baby's name was "Nine Twenty-two" when Elizabeth introduced her to her at home.

This was very much like how Six-thirty had been adopted. Elizabeth and Six-thirty experienced joy for the first time in months when they realized they would soon be a family of three again.

## CHAPTER 17: THE HARRIET SLOANE

*All-New Cast*

- Harriet Sloane: Elizabeth's wise older neighbor

Elizabeth found it difficult to handle a new mother's responsibilities, including cooking, cleaning, changing diapers, burping, and putting the baby to bed. Elizabeth, whose world revolved around logic and reason, was baffled by her baby's unpredictable needs and refusal to adhere to her established routine.

Her new business of completing ex-colleagues jobs for money wasn't enough to support a child, so she opted out of anesthetic during labor.

One morning, Dr. Boryweitz showed up needing Elizabeth's assistance as he met with Donatti; after she aided him, she went on to perform her work but eventually fell from tiredness.

In her dream, Elizabeth was reading a book with Calvin. During her reading, she remarked on the difficulty of fiction. She claimed that the story could contain elements of dramatic irony and a fourth-wall break, but it was impossible to know.

Elizabeth's next-door neighbor, Harriet Sloane, discovered her dozing on the floor. She checked on Elizabeth and then changed the baby.

The name Madeline appeared here for the first time.

Elizabeth's laboratory in the place of the kitchen and her scientific approach to brewing coffee both astonished Harriet. Harriet recognized the book on child care that Elizabeth had purchased and remarked on the irony of it being authored by a guy. Elizabeth and Harriet agreed with her theory that he had written it under the pretense that his wife had done the work.

A mother of four, Harriet told it like it was; she described infants as "horrible," "a devil," and "a gremlin" (Garmus, 2022, pp. 142-145). She gave Elizabeth an honest assessment of motherhood, explaining that it's not all rainbows and unicorns and that it's normal to want to give your baby away when things get tough. Harriet's last counsel was to "take a moment every day to tend to your own needs," but she never did. She invited Elizabeth to phone her whenever she needed anything and sent over a meal she had made.

Forcing Elizabeth's hand seemed the only way to get her to accept assistance. Even though Elizabeth didn't particularly want Harriet's aid, she couldn't deny her gratitude.

## CHAPTER 18: LEGALLY MAD

*All-New Cast*

- Harriet's chauvinist husband, Mr. Sloane

Harriet, like everyone else, initially assumed Calvin and Elizabeth's relationship was superficial and predicated solely on Elizabeth's appearances. However, as she observed the couple's interactions over time, she came to recognize them as true soulmates.

Unlike these women, Harriet did not love her husband. He made lewd remarks about Elizabeth, pleasured himself in public next to Harriet, and had no qualms about pursuing other women. Harriet didn't think much of herself, but she thought Mr. Sloane was very repulsive.

After Calvin passed away, Harriet stood across the street and observed all the male visitors to Elizabeth's home with great interest. When she read Chapter 17, "Elizabeth on the Floor," she realized she was being just as critical as Mr. Sloane and decided to pay a visit.

Harriet then made a covert plea for Elizabeth to contact her.

Elizabeth thought back to the moment she had dug into a nurse's arm while screaming in agony during labor. Same nurse checked in to see how she was doing afterwards. Calvin's murder may have been avoided, and Elizabeth was upset at him for lying to get money for her research. So she went to the nurse and declared her sanity void. It's possible that the nurse's arm injury was still bothering her, so she scrawled "Mad" on the paper.

A birth certificate, proving that the newborn's name was "legally Mad" (Garmus, 2022, p. 154) at last. Elizabeth hoped that the sight of her newborn would inspire a name, but it didn't. She attempted a legal name change, but was stopped when she was asked for identifying information such as a marriage certificate. Before she realized that "Mad" had stuck, she attempted several other names.

At the chapter's end, Elizabeth demonstrates growth in character by calling Harriet.

## CHAPTER 19: DECEMBER 1956

One year later, Madeline was practicing her newfound ability to speak by repeating phrases. Six-thirty took the role of her guardian and vowed to ensure that her loved ones were safe at all costs.

Madeline was raised unconventionally by her mother, Elizabeth, who promoted risky exploration and discovery under the guise of "experimental learning" (Garmus, 2022, p.157).

Dr. Mason came to visit as he had promised to do after Madeline was born. He inquired about her children, her erging, and whether or not she had any assistance. He began washing dishes and folding diapers while chatting and noted he still had a free chair in one of his rows. She feigned preoccupation, and he responded that they row in the morning.

Elizabeth was sad because she knew she and Calvin had discussed not having children, but she also knew he would have been a wonderful father. Madeline and Elizabeth were learning from each other despite Madeline's frequent fears that she was failing at being a mother as a single parent. Madeline's ability to find magic in everyday occurrences astounded Elizabeth.

Madeline will be a rower, Dr. Mason reaffirmed. He also saw that she had the ability to interpret others' expressions and gestures. He mentioned a new rowing coach and how he'd told him about Elizabeth, but he didn't specify whether the coach knew that Elizabeth was a woman.

He and Calvin were both utterly dedicated to their rowing. Because of Mason, she asked Harriet to watch the kids at 4:30 a.m. so she could go rowing with him. Harriet accepted unexpectedly because she longed for freedom from Mr. Sloane.

The rowers and their coach looked annoyed by her presence. After their argument, Mason tried to reassure her that everything was fine, but she didn't believe him. When she was having terrible contractions during labor, he would say things weren't "so bad," a euphemism for "very bad" (Garmus, 2022, p. 165).

Despite her fatigue, she was happy to return to the water and rowing. Mason said parenting children was similar to rowing in that you could only look back at your past acts and never know what was in store for you.

# CHAPTER 20: LIFE STORY

*New characters*

- Mrs. Mudford: Madeline's conservative teacher

Madeline, who was almost four and growing taller and smarter every day, had trouble communicating with others who were like her mother and couldn't do simple things like tie her shoes. Elizabeth enrolled her in kindergarten so she might meet other children of a similar age. Elizabeth altered Madeline's birth certificate so that she would be a year older and therefore eligible for admission.

Harriet enjoyed having Madeline around and was sad to see her leave because of this. Six-thirty felt the same way because he couldn't keep an eye on Madeline while she was at school.

Madeline drew a chalk picture depicting her "life story" (Garmus, 2022, p. 170) that included images of her mother rowing, the sun, the moon, flowers, Six o'clock, and other things. There was a spiral in the center that was dubbed "the pit of death" (Garmus, 2022, p. 170). Elizabeth's ability to "read" people, as Mason put it, was on display in the mournful picture she drew of her mother.

In the end, Elizabeth was able to find the time to start looking for work because Madeline was attending school. They were having financial difficulties, and she had already reversed their mortgage to borrow money. She was relieved to learn that she and Calvin wouldn't need to rely on welfare anymore after discovering that Calvin had put her name on the deed.

Given their predicament, she had little choice but to go against Harriet's advice and apply for a position at Hastings again.

Donatti was relieved that Calvin and Elizabeth had left, but the lack of progress on abiogenesis enraged the anonymous backer. He had to choose between losing the man's financial support and having to hire Elizabeth again. Boryweitz appeared to make headway, but it turned out that everything he knew came from chatting to Elizabeth.

He had no choice but to hire her.

## CHAPTER 21: E.Z.

Hastings gave Elizabeth a new lab coat with "E.Z." instead of "E. Zott" stitched on the back when she returned. It was designed to sound like "easy," a derogatory term for a sexually available woman.

Dr. Boryweitz was the only person who knew that Elizabeth was still working on abiogenesis, but Donatti claimed that Elizabeth had caught him looking through her files during one of his visits, so he knew. Donatti remarked that he was shortly to have an article published on a rather dull subject.

He said she would be starting as a lab technician, and neither her prior position nor her salary would be restored. He insulted her with the name "Luscious" (Garmus, 2022, p. 174) and said that she would no longer receive the "special treatment" she had previously. Before she could respond, he assured her they would fund her graduate studies, adding that it was merely an online typing tutorial.

When Elizabeth saw Miss Frask in the restroom, she stormed in and barricaded herself in a stall beside her. The reader learns that after four years, Frask still hasn't been promoted and is now reporting to a clueless college boy who told her to slim down.

They had an argument in which Frask made a sarcastic apology for Elizabeth's decision to have a daughter rather than a son. Madeline's daycare instructor, Mrs. Mudford, disapproved when she asked for a blue item instead of a pink one.

Miss Frask unwittingly informed Elizabeth of the wealthy benefactor behind the abiogenesis project. She disclosed that Elizabeth was portrayed to the donor as a man and suggested they were romantically linked.

Elizabeth's discovery that Miss Frask was an "almost-psychologist" (Garmus, 2022, p. 178), during their argument, led to both of them admitting that their advisers had sexually attacked them, preventing them from completing their PhDs.

## CHAPTER 22: THE PRESENT

Elizabeth and Miss Frask developed an unintentional friendship while at Hastings. Frask could not locate any information for Elizabeth regarding the sponsor's background. During their lunch, Frask informed Elizabeth calmly and without emotion that she had been sacked due to her failure to lose weight. Elizabeth advised her to take legal action against the unlawful termination, but Frask said there was no need because she could find other work as a typist.

According to Chapter 12, Frask sent Elizabeth a gift from Calvin's discarded possessions. Even though they knew it was wrong, they helped themselves to the boxes.

Two women mistreated by Hastings, their professors, and the world had more in common than they realized.

# CHAPTER 23: KCTV STUDIOS

*Changes and updates to the cast*

- Mr. Wakely: Calvin's religious, surfer ex-pen pal
- Tommy Dixon: Madeline's classmate who thinks her family is poor

After two months on the job, Elizabeth realized she was vastly overqualified for and bored with her low-paying position. Donatti's paper published that month, was a direct copy of her work. Donatti had photocopied her paperwork on the day she was rehired, and Boryweitz had noticed and done nothing about it.

Donatti published it to appease the dissatisfied investor with "Mr. Zott's" performance; the investor had no idea she had been sacked years prior.

When Elizabeth entered Donatti's office, he was barely paying attention. But because of his commitments to the investor, he couldn't make her resign, so she did so on the spot.

When Elizabeth got home, Harriet and their kid were waiting for her. Harriet would take Madeline to school, have Six Thirty pick her up, and then take care of Madeline again until Elizabeth got home from work.

Madeline was disappointed when her classmates rejected her sailing knots and an arrowhead for show-and-tell. She would go outside in the pouring rain to tie the knots as if preparing for the world's end. After her father's passing, she realized she must always be on guard.

Madeline's "inappropriate questions" (Garmus, 2022, p. 188) prompted Elizabeth to have multiple conversations with Madeline's teacher. After hearing a youngster at school, Tommy Dixon, say they had no money, Madeline asked if it was confirmed during supper.

At this, Elizabeth recalled the contents of the Hastings box she had taken, titled "Rowing." There were numerous job offers inside, many of which paid more than Calvin's current position at Hastings. When she did, she discovered letters from all the fictitious family members, including one "mother" who offered to donate to his studies rather than accept any of his stolen funds.

In a folder labeled "Wakely," she discovered letters written to him by his former pen buddy some ten years earlier. Mr. Wakely, a devout surfer, corresponded with Calvin on the subject of God's and science's coexistence. The two argued back and forth as Calvin flatly rejected the idea. Wakely wrote that the weather in Commons was beautiful. Elizabeth figured out the ideal rowing weather was why Calvin worked in the Commons.

Calvin appeared to have persuaded Wakely that religion was not dissimilar from trusting in more straightforward moral lessons found in fairy tales. When Wakely noted that he came from a long line of ministers and inquired about Calvin's father, the latter responded in all capital letters that he despised his paternal ancestor and fervently wished for his demise. Elizabeth was taken aback. Based on what he told her in Chapter 5, she assumed his father had passed away in a railway accident.

In the present, Walter Pine, a TV producer, was having trouble filling the afternoon slot, which was crucial to his livelihood. Days earlier, Elizabeth had confronted him about his daughter stealing lunch. Because he was divorced and worked long hours, Amanda frequently brought intoxicating beverages or other items in her lunchbox.

After the encounter, his thoughts kept returning to Elizabeth, and he called her several times before Madeline picked up. He discussed with Elizabeth the potential for a KCTV cookery show where she would star. There was no waiting list, and the pay was excellent. Despite her misgivings, she agreed.

# CHAPTER 24: THE AFTERNOON ZONE OF DEPRESSION

*All-New Cast*

- Phil Lebensmal, the harsh and overbearing superior of Walter Pine

Elizabeth was unhappy about wearing the tight clothes that Walter's employer, Phil Lebensmal, insisted upon when she went for her wardrobe fitting. In addition to having Elizabeth mix a cocktail at the end of each episode, Phil wanted her to be an objectified and sexualized housewife who appealed to men's vision of the perfect woman. Walter resisted at first, but under Phil's leadership, he eventually gave in.

Elizabeth refused to wear the outfits and proposed a compromise in which she would wear a lab coat instead. Thinking about Phil's requests, Walter said no. He couldn't understand Elizabeth's desire to experiment with the lab coat and evaluate the findings.

Walter approved of the TV set, which he knew Elizabeth would hate because it was characteristic of a stay-at-home wife's kitchen. On the other hand, Elizabeth insisted on chemistry-related updates and equipment like Bunsen burners and a steel countertop.

Walter described the concept of the Afternoon Depression Zone to Elizabeth after she complained that cooking wasn't "fun" (Garmus, 2022). Between one and five in the afternoon, people are at their least productive and most half-asleep. Except for housewives, who had to rush through their chores before dinner? Walter suggested watching mindless television in the afternoon, relaxing the mind and rousing its tired inhabitants. He emphasized the need to be engaging because the show aired at 4:30 p.m. when the Zone was winding down and people were beginning to prepare dinner.

Walter mentioned having a good time at a dinner party and naturally thought that she and "Mr. Zott" would throw such events. Elizabeth set him straight by stating that she was never married, and when he assumed this was due to an affair, she clarified that she did not wish to get married. He warned her that sharing the news with others would be unwise. She broke the news that Calvin had died to Walter, and he comforted her as best he could.

She brought up the end of his marriage, which he claimed had never been motivated by love. Also, to his dismay, he had just lately learned that he was not Amanda's biological father.

They became fast friends because of their shared experience with Walter's mother, Mrs. Mudford, who was persuaded that, because he was a single parent, Walter was a pedophile.

They were more candid and honest with one other than Walter had ever been with anybody else. An improbable bond blossomed between them.

Elizabeth stressed that she would not lie to Phil and portray herself as someone other than a scientist.

This brash nature, which Walter assumes will be her undoing, is actually the secret to her success.

## CHAPTER 25: THE AVERAGE JANE

*All-New Cast*

- Rosa: Elizabeth's make-up and hair artist

The show's premiere could have been a success. Although following orders had never been Elizabeth's strong suit, she had practiced reading from the cue cards as Walter had directed.

She came onto the stage but looked about for the first time rather than following the cues to begin the performance. A phony window, several sewing machines, a cookie jar, and a Jesus statue completed the illusion of a typical housewife's kitchen. She spoke to Walter in real time about how terrible it was.

Walter yelled at her to stay on the script as commercials played to limit the damage. Even though she insisted that the set be altered, he emphasized that it was designed with what the "average" lady in mind had in mind. She proclaimed her femininity and her disdain for it.

The word "fun" on the cue cards halted her reading after the intermission (Garmus, 2022, p. 216). After a short pause, she regained her composure and deviated from the script. She took the frivolous decorations out of her office, declared that she was serious about her profession, and understood the challenges that mothers and wives face. A housewife, somewhere, overheard this on TV and decided to listen.

Rosa, Elizabeth's stylist, tried to lighten the mood after the show by praising the pencil work in Elizabeth's hair as Phil was scolding Walter. While Elizabeth enjoyed the episode, Phil was left disappointed.

She claimed she couldn't read the cards when she meant that she was too proud to admit that she was wrong when Walter rebuked her.

An assistant cut in to explain they were getting phone calls from people who had seen the broadcast and wanted to know more about a chemical substance. Elizabeth revealed that the liquid in question was vinegar and said she had the inspiration for the next episode's list of necessities while filming.

The fact that Walter had never received phone calls for any of his previous shows tempered his anger at Elizabeth's capricious changes.

## CHAPTER 26: THE FUNERAL

After arguing with Elizabeth over and over again, Walter finally made her film an episode in front of a live audience so she would be forced to stick to the script.

But first, she threw some of the set pieces into the crowd for the spectators to grab and handed out the rest. As Walter tried to settle down, she improvised a description of the constituent parts of spinach.

She tried to hurl things into the crowd during the live broadcast to get the audience involved, she revealed enthusiastically during a commercial break. He did not find it funny at all.

He willingly imagined his own burial as she returned to the stage. The mourners dressed in primary hues, with some relaying the tedious details of his demise. His eulogy, which Elizabeth was reading, was crazily uplifting and encouraging. The final words spoken by Elizabeth on the television snapped him back to reality: "Children, set the table." Garmus (2022), quoting Chapter 17's Harriet, tells her daughter, "Your mother needs a moment to herself" (p. 226).

Rosa and Elizabeth found Walter after he had passed out from lack of food and stress. Elizabeth presented the dish that she had prepared on the program. Although he declined, Elizabeth still left the spinach in his car because she knew his kid didn't like it. He was so worn out that he had to take it home with him. When they finally had a bite, Amanda proclaimed it to be the best meal she'd ever had.

## CHAPTER 27: ALL ABOUT ME

In May of 1960, Madeline and her classmates were assigned a family tree project to help them get to know one another better. Mrs. Mudford clashed with Madeline, who believed people were animals, while she tried convincing them to assume it was about themselves. The result was complete anarchy in the classroom. Discipline was restored after Mudford threatened to call the school principal. Because of her "humans are animals" remark, she kept Madeline out of the house passed her bedtime.

Harriet sought to teach Madeline the importance of agreeing politely with others, even if they were wrong, while at home. When Mudford said that God created everything, and Madeline refused to accept her, Madeline struggled to make sense of this. In response to Madeline's inquiry about Harriet's religious beliefs, Harriet confirmed that she was a God-fearing Christian. She hoped Mr. Sloane would go to hell so she could send him there.

Madeline presented Harriet with the family tree, and Harriet voiced her concern that doing so forced one to define oneself about another. Madeline didn't know much about her father, so a family portrait with him was essential, despite Harriet's warnings that she shouldn't reveal it to Elizabeth. Despite her repeated visits, the librarian had ignored her request for his school's yearbooks.

When listing Calvin's relatives, Harriet makes a mistake and calls her his "godmother" (Garmus, 2022, p. 232). She knew of this so-called godmother since she'd wandered around his house before him meeting Elizabeth when he'd left his front door open in a panic. She started to close it, but then she became curious and found a request for donations from his former boys' home that he'd thrown out.

Currently, Harriet is in the process of enlightening Madeline on the meaning of a godmother. By "fairy godmother," she had meant the wealthy benefactor who had funded All Saints' operations. Since most donors favored anonymity—which Madeline mistook for secrecy—she cautioned against adding him to her family tree. When Madeline questioned Harriet if she had ever kept a secret, she falsely said she had not.

Madeline's peculiar hobbies and pursuits astonished Harriet. For example, she liked to read dense literature and learn about natural disasters. Madeline's outstanding abilities, according to Harriet, were the result of Elizabeth's persistent efforts to have her little daughter become literate. Even Harriet picked up some helpful chemistry knowledge from Elizabeth's show, so she'd discovered a way to inject some seriousness and inspiration into the kitchen.

The six-month trial run of Supper at Six was coming to a close, and Elizabeth worried it would be canceled. However, Madeline mentioned to Harriet that some children at school had lunches like hers because their parents watched the show.

The show allowed Elizabeth to compensate Harriet for her babysitting services. Elizabeth was unwavering in her convictions, even after Harriet advised her to appease Phil to preserve her work.

Although Harriet thought men needed special attention due to their "fragile egos" (Garmus, 2022, p. 23 7), Elizabeth treated men the way she would have liked to be treated: as equals.

Elizabeth met with Mrs. Mudford about Madeline not wanting to undertake stereotypical girl things. Mudford claims that Madeline was interested in joining the boys on "safety patrol" (Garmus, 2022, p. The lads were especially offended by the fact that Madeline was the tallest student in class.

When Elizabeth told Harriet that this strengthened her resolve never to undervalue herself or her abilities to make men feel better, Harriet said nothing.

Harriet's ostensibly obligatory religious observance was examined, as was the atheism of Madeline and Elizabeth. Madeline represents the imposition of these conventions on impressionable young minds, whereas Elizabeth represents the overturning of these traditions by showing women that they need not be constrained by their gender.

# CHAPTER 28: SAINTS

*Changes to the Cast*

- Calvin's non-religious pen friend, the Reverend Wakely

Madeline researched the boys' home where her father spent his formative years by visiting the city library. According to Harriet, the sender was aware that the given address was in Iowa and that the given name sounded "girlish" (Garmus, 2022, p.

Madeline and the librarian were having a conversation when a preacher overheard them and chimed in with some advice. Since caring for orphans was so challenging, he posited, religious institutions were commonly named after various saints. Madeline was compiling a family tree, and he shared Harriet's opinion that it was meaningless because a person's identity is not determined by their family's history.

Madeline believed that the workers at the orphanage would be the closest thing her father had to a family, but the minister worried that, given his past, many of them were actually pedophiles.

He realized the irony of his position when he realized he had to repeatedly tell them they would have better times ahead even though he knew otherwise.

The minister never talked down to her or patronized her in any way, and he was the only person who consistently referred to her as "Mad" rather than "Madeline." In sharp contrast to her earlier exchange with Harriet, he revealed that he, too, was a secret keeper.

He identified himself as Wakely and was instrumental in assisting Madeline in locating the name of the institution. She couldn't engage her mother or make any long-distance phone calls because there was only a contact number posted. When she revealed that her father was his old pen pal Calvin Evans, Wakely volunteered to call them for her.

When Wakely was a student at Harvard, he enrolled in a chemistry course to disprove evolution and prove that God created everything. But in the end, he had to disprove his own convictions, which presented a challenge in his study of religion.

One evening he attended a panel discussion featuring researchers like Calvin Evans. Calvin didn't say much, but he did use religion as an example of something that is permanent and significant but lacks vitality. Because of this, Wakely decided to start pen palling with Calvin.

They started off debating God and science but eventually moved on to more personal matters, such as fathers, where Calvin responded strongly while Wakely was at a loss for words.

Unfortunately, Wakely's father passed away shortly after he received his diploma. After his father's death, Wakely remained in the Commons and assumed his position as minister. He later discovered that Calvin had resided in the same city, but tragically, Calvin had passed away before they could finally meet. Wakely decided to pay his respects by offering to preside over his burial.

It was fate that brought him face to face with Calvin's daughter; he had seen Elizabeth and Six-thirty at the burial but never had the chance to introduce himself.

Madeline came upon the photo of her mother and Six-thirty in the newspaper article about Calvin's burial. Since Madeline was technically present due to Elizabeth's pregnancy, she claimed the picture as her own.

Madeline requested Wakely to keep a secret from anyone else before she departed. She told him something, and he told her something, both of which the reader doesn't know about.

Readers are given the opportunity to explore and gradually uncover knowledge together with Madeline by withholding details regarding Calvin's background when he was alive. An emotional impact is produced because of the revelation that Madeline is emotionally distant from Calvin and needs more information in order to feel connected to him, much like Calvin did with his biological father, albeit under very different circumstances.

## CHAPTER 29: BONDING

During another Supper at Six, Elizabeth discussed the various types of chemical bonding. She made simple analogies, like marriages, to make her points. Attendees and viewers at home jotted down her every word.

She equated ionic bonding to the premise of opposites attract, like the marriage of two radically different persons who were nonetheless closely bonded. A covalent bond is when two people complement each other well, like when they bring food and wine to a dinner party. The hydrogen bond was likened to love at first sight; it was intense but readily shattered, like when a person in a new relationship learns something unflattering about their partner.

A mother's newfound chemistry expertise served as the basis for an impassioned plea to her daughter to continue her studies despite opposition from her boyfriend. This proved that Elizabeth had sown the seeds of transformation, prompting women throughout the United States to reevaluate their expectations for their daughters and themselves.

However, Walter could only keep the show going if Elizabeth complied with Phil's demands. Elizabeth's unconventional pedagogy drew criticism from viewers, but she was unmoved by Walter's demands to adjust the show.

As much as Walter detested Elizabeth's use of scientific jargon, she made Rosa and the other women in the audience feel strong and "capable" (Garmus, 2022, p. 255). Walter was bothered by Rosa's use of the technical term for aspirin and Elizabeth's choice to wear trousers.

The show and Amanda's family tree project were constant sources of anxiety for him. It emphasized blood ties, which he and she lacked, and demanded a photo of her with her deceased mother.

When Elizabeth asked Walter for fire extinguishers during the upcoming chemistry lecture, he completely ignored her.

Elizabeth completed the chicken pot pie she had been making, likening its complexity to a well-oiled civilization like Sweden. To the dismay of the videographer, she opened the floor for questions from the live audience. A woman spoke up and said she'd always wished she could go to medical school to become an open-heart surgeon but couldn't. Elizabeth urged her to follow her passions despite being a full-time mother of four. They congratulated her, and Elizabeth handed her a chicken pot pie as part of her "Free Day" initiative (which she claimed Walter had conceptualized).

In addition to chemistry, Elizabeth taught her listeners about the benefits of government-subsidized childcare and relocating to Sweden to improve their quality of life. She pushed against convention by showing women they could achieve everything they set their minds to, regardless of what society had told them they were capable of.

## CHAPTER 30: 99 PERCENT

Madeline had submitted her work, which included a newspaper clipping, a family tree featuring numerous historical personalities, and a nut representing the "fairy godmother" who sponsors All Saints. The fact that people were 99 percent similar was also noted (Garmus, 2022, p. 262). To help Madeline get a more precise percentage, Elizabeth tried teaching her about decimals instead than lecturing her on other topics.

Harriet gave Elizabeth a log of voicemails. Both were magazines; she ignored the one from Wakely and read the LA Times. The latter requested an interview, but Elizabeth turned them down because their interests lay more in food than science.

Madeline inquired as to whether or not anything was wrong and if she could learn more about her father. Nothing was wrong, Elizabeth assured her, and she had already filled her in on Calvin. Madeline inquired if something awful had happened to her, too, but Elizabeth didn't hear her, and Elizabeth speculated that Calvin was being secretive about his time in the boys' home because of his trauma.

Walter called Elizabeth to tell her that the Madeline-like project his daughter had worked on had yet to go over well with Mrs. Mudford. Next year, Mrs. Mudford will be Madeline's teacher again, and Elizabeth intended to complain. Elizabeth also wanted to file a complaint against him, as Walter had stated Phil's dissatisfaction. Walter suggested she include the consumption of a specific brand of soup on the show to attract sponsors and hopefully get Phil to leave them alone.

The following day, word quickly circulated that Madeline's parents were never married, Tommy's dad was an alcoholic, and Amanda didn't have a mother because of the family tree assignment. All of this was fodder for Mudford's tittle-tattle with the moms.

Elizabeth learned the next day that her salary was much lower than the men who worked beside her. As she had already known, Harriet had been the victim of Mr. Sloane's physical abuse. If Elizabeth hurt him, the police would blame her. Therefore, Harriet discouraged her from calling them.

Later in the show, as everyone was taking notes, Elizabeth threw out the canned soup Walter had instructed her to use and gave a sober explanation of the several types of poisonous mushrooms. After the show concluded, Rosa told her that she and Walter had to part ways since Rosa was worried about Phil and needed to chat alone. It's okay, according to Elizabeth.

Phil reprimanded her for the show's criticisms and low ratings in his office. When she didn't respond how he wanted, he threatened her employment and ended up terminating her and the rest of the cast. Elizabeth did not react emotionally to his attempts at intimidation or power.

He wanted a presentation that reinforced "societal norms" (Garmus, 2022, p. 274); she wanted to inspire rational thought and a sense of community among individuals who live in a culture that devalues individuality. She added that Walter wasn't to blame, even though he had pressured her to comply with Phil's wishes.

In the preceding two hours, Phil had smoked a cigarette, consumed two shots of whiskey, and taken ten alkalizer tablets. She calmly pulled out a long, sharp knife to defend herself, and just as he was about to try to assault her sexually, he passed out.

# CHAPTER 31: THE GET-WELL CARD

Phil suffered a heart attack and was taken to the hospital. Walter was frantic to find out why Elizabeth had dialed 911 that night. He knew Phil was a nasty man and never wanted anyone to meet with him alone, but he also knew he'd done nothing to stop men like Phil in the past.

She explained that he had dismissed her, him, and the rest of the cast because Walter had "failed to rein [her] in" (Garmus, 2022, p. 279). Even while Walter would love it if she read the cue cards he created and wore the tight clothes he bought for her, he said he never made her. He said he did his best to get on Phil's good side by complying with his requests because that was how things were done.

Despite Phil warning him that their sponsors would depart and that the audience loathed her, the truth was that the show had more viewer involvement than any other show, such as fan mail and calls.

He was devastated when she told Walter what had happened that night and that Phil had attempted to abuse her.

She showed Walter the various advertisements and sponsorship offers she found when searching Phil's office after calling for an ambulance. Some of these plans included putting the show into syndication allowing it to be broadcast on networks other than Commons.

After a few days, Walter replaced Phil at work. Elizabeth urged him to use his newfound authority for good, even if it meant acting the part. So he did, and he told everyone that Elizabeth had saved Phil's life, which resulted in many sponsorship arrangements.

He commissioned a Get Well Soon card depicting Phil with his heart held aloft like a football. Some people wished him well, while others swore and cursed at him in their messages. Rosa's reassuring words to Elizabeth days after the attack and the death, except for a note from Phil's secretary, suggest that this wasn't his first time assaulting someone.

Walter wrote in the card that he hoped Phil never recovered after years of blindly following Phil's directions and doing nothing about his reprehensible behavior.

## CHAPTER 32: MEDIUM RARE

*All-New Cast*

- In the parking lot of KCTV, you'll find Seymour Browne.

Madeline's teacher, Mrs. Mudford, returned for the following school year, and since Harriet knew Elizabeth would disapprove, she let and even encouraged Madeline to skip class. Harriet made a fake note, and they headed off to watch Supper at Six in concert. The problem was that when they arrived, hundreds of other people had the same idea and were waiting in line, too. No parking was available, so the attendant sent them away.

He had tried to discourage them and mentioned that he had been yelled at numerous times. Madeline anticipated Elizabeth's displeasure and asked him to sign his name in the notebook bearing her name. But as soon as he saw her name, he knew she was the TV host's offspring.

Harriet and Madeline had entered and taken seats at the front of the auditorium. Madeline was overjoyed to see her mother in this light but also envious that she had to share her with such an attentive audience.

Harriet and Madeline were dragged into Walter's office during a commercial break, where he revealed they weren't welcome since Elizabeth had asked him to keep Madeline out of sight now that the program and Elizabeth were so successful.

He reflected on the fact that Elizabeth was his best friend and, because of their close relationship, he was aware of her depression despite the show's success.

When Madeline inquired why her mother was so well-known, Walter said she was uncommonly forthright and honest. At the same time, Elizabeth answered a question from the crowd regarding whether or not she prays before meals by reiterating that she is an atheist, in keeping with Walter's earlier assertion.

## CHAPTER 33: FAITH

After Elizabeth's comments, Walter got numerous calls of outrage, including threats of violence and the loss of sponsors. The incoherence of this action baffled Elizabeth. If they could appreciate her nonbelief, she reasoned, why couldn't they respect her respect for their faith in God? Things weren't so cut and dry, though, because individuals were irrational and inconsistent. This was evident not only in issues of religion but also sexism and homophobia.

Miss Frasier watched the show while on the clock when the following episode aired. Reverend Wakely had hired her on as a typist. Elizabeth spoke out in support of Rosa Parks and the civil rights movement, explaining that she believed discrimination to be absurd because every person's DNA was almost identical.

A woman in the audience asked her what she could consume in addition to her diet pills to speed up her weight loss. Instead of taking the medicines, Elizabeth recommended rowing, which made her think of Calvin.

Madeline ran into Wakely again at the park, this time with the latter in shock after seeing her mother on TV. He told her that he was able to reach All Saints, but that they did not have any records pertaining to Calvin Evans. Madeline was confident it was the right house and that they had lied, but he was convinced it wasn't.

## CHAPTER 34: ALL SAINTS

*All-new & improved cartoons*

- Wilson: the wealthy benefactor who contributed to the Parker Foundation's support of the orphanage.
- Leader of the Parker Foundation, Avery Parker

In the first part of the chapter, set in 1933, a bishop is sent to a boys' home as a form of penance for insulting the archbishop, with the promise that he will be granted a better opportunity if he can maintain financial support. Four years later, he still hadn't found an endowment—a gift of funds to support the home—despite his best efforts.

In the present day, when a caller asked about Calvin Evans (Wakely), the bishop told his secretary to tell the caller that Calvin Evans had never resided in that area. If the caller persisted, he instructed the secretary to state that Calvin Evans had been at another house when it burned down.

He recalled how, many years ago, nobody seemed to care that Calvin was constantly getting into mischief until a man named Wilson from a big Catholic organization showed along. The bishop lied and said Calvin was deceased when Wilson asked whether he may visit some living relatives. The bishop lied to ensure the school would get a donation in Calvin's name. Wilson was distraught at the news and gave a donation to Calvin's "memorial fund" (Garmus, 2022, p. 302).

When the foundation's head, Avery Parker, learned that Calvin was still alive after all these years, he threatened legal action against the residence because of Calvin's newfound fame.

Again, Wakely posed as a potential British sponsor with an interest in Calvin Evan's former orphanage. He was ironically lying to uncover the truth. Wakely and the bishop discussed the phony donation, but the bishop swore that Calvin Evans had never attended All Saints before Wakely brought up the sum of money in question. It was hilarious that the bishop's favorite show, Supper at Six, was about to begin, so he hurried to reveal the fact that Calvin had grown up in that area and that a memorial fund had been established in his honor.

When they next saw each other, Wakely had caught Madeline up to speed, but she had already shown her wit and intelligence by asking why a memorial fund was being established for her father nine years before his death. Wakely had assumed it was a memorial fund established in Calvin's name before his passing, but he dismissed her concern and handed her the Parker Foundation's post office box number nevertheless.

## CHAPTER 35: THE SMELL OF FAILURE

Elizabeth noticed a large group of women assembling near the boathouse on her way to the docks. When Elizabeth on the show advised rowing as a form of exercise, women all around the country took notice and began taking lessons.

After years of attempting to persuade his wife to row, Dr. Mason was annoyed that Elizabeth had done it in a single statement. For days, he called Elizabeth to complain that his laboring patients were too engrossed in her show to push.

Anti-atheist protestors gathered in the KCTV parking lot to voice their displeasure at Elizabeth's nonbelief. Walter didn't tell her about the death threats since he knew she'd rather deal with them alone.

At home, Six-thirty saw an unsatisfied viewer who didn't applaud at the show's end. He rode in on a vehicle and pretended to be dead to fool security guard Seymour into letting him into the KCTV studios. Seymour mistook Six-thirty for Harriet and Madeline and told Elizabeth they had all secretly attended the play months earlier.

Walter lied and said Madeline had to see her mother working on a school project when she challenged him. Walter agreed to have Six-thirty on the show without even realizing it.

Everyone, besides Walter, rapidly began to love the hour of 6:30. Many episodes later, Sixthirty searched the audience for the one glum spectator he'd spotted before. He saw her among the crowd and approached it, only to be overcome by the scent of nitroglycerin, a reminder of the bombs he had been compelled to uncover many years before. Despite his shock, he reached into the woman's suitcase and placed the handmade explosive on Seymour's desk.

After Seymour rescued the studio, he was acclaimed as a hero. The same reporter who covered Calvin's funeral also covered this story, expressing shock that a cookery show was the target of murder and bomb threats.

## CHAPTER 36: LIFE AND DEATH

*Fresh faces*

- Franklin Roth: a reporter at Life magazine

Walter told his daughter during one of his numerous dinners with her that Life magazine wanted to profile Elizabeth on the front cover. Elizabeth initially said no, but then Walter said he'd also called Chemistry Today, where Calvin was featured.

He angered Elizabeth by saying they weren't looking for a TV show chef. After Walter wounded Elizabeth, he opened up to Harriet, sharing how much he and Amanda loved her.

Harriet manipulated the situation so that Elizabeth would agree to the interview behind the scenes. Franklin Roth, a magazine reporter, was told to gloss over Calvin Evans's contributions and concentrate instead on Elizabeth's. He sat among the live audience and conducted interviews with some of the predominantly female spectators. One viewer remarked that the show gave her the impression that she was "being taken seriously" (Garmus, 2022, p. 323), while another predicted that men couldn't handle ever having to play the role of a woman.

Elizabeth's interview responses to Roth's comments on her clothes and hairstyle needed to be more cordial. She gave him a chilly answer when he asked about the pencil in her hair. Elizabeth invited him and the photographer to her house so that she could be more comfortable.

She showed them the erg and explained how helpful Sixty was in her home laboratory. She detailed her abiogenesis research, piqued even non-scientist Roth's curiosity, but ultimately decided to abandon it. He persisted in his questioning by bringing up Calvin.

Her perception that he cared more about Calvin's work than her own crushed her. Roth felt terrible about asking and wanted to apologize, but he didn't. She did the unexpected and told him the truth about her family, Dr. Meyers' assault, Donatti's plagiarism, and Calvin's untimely demise.

## CHAPTER 37: SOLD OUT

At the outset of his essay, Roth referred to Elizabeth as "the most influential, intelligent person on television" (Garmus, 2022, p.329).

Elizabeth reflected on how she and Calvin were meant to be and how Calvin regarded her work as equally essential as his own in the interview, noting that Donatti plagiarized her in its entirety in his most recent paper.

She said that teaching chemistry to girls and women helped them see the atomic basis of the societal constraints placed on them. She implied that believers could remain uninformed and avoid responsibility for their actions by praying instead of taking the initiative to make things better themselves.

The rest of her life fell apart; she was molested in college, her parents were con artists, and her brother committed suicide.

It was also revealed that Calvin had a rough upbringing, what with the loss of his parents and aunt and the violence he suffered at the boys' home. She didn't say that she knew from Calvin's childhood diary that his lifelong resentment was against his father.

Elizabeth revealed to Roth that she held sole responsibility for Calvin's passing. She was ashamed that her fraud of a father had inspired her to give up her studies for Donatti, enroll Madeline in a school where she thought she didn't belong, and become a "performer" (Garmus, 2022, p. 334).

Roth opted to write about abiogenesis instead of repeating what she had already said. In the first sentence of his work, his editor substituted the word "attractive" for "intelligent" (Garmus, 2022, p. 335).

He had compiled remarks from her father, Dr. Meyers, Donatti, and Mrs. Mudford, all of whom had been critical of her. Her father had branded her the "devil's spawn," Meyers had said she was "more interested in men than molecules," and Mudford had termed her "disruptive" to her daughter's wellbeing because she didn't conform to the traditional role of a woman (Garmus, 2022, p. 335).

Thanks to Mudford, Roth also published Madeline's family tree in the piece. Madeline's addition of Walter to the tree caused a rift between Elizabeth and him, as did the depiction of Harriet poisoning her husband, the gravestone of Madeline's father, and the fabricated connections between her and historical characters.

## CHAPTER 38: BROWNIES

After the demeaning magazine came out in July 1961, Walter tried to cheer Elizabeth up by offering her a chemical toy for girls and other forms of advertising. She was enthusiastic until he revealed its intended use as a perfume ingredient and its characteristic pink color.

A few episodes later, Elizabeth had planned to talk about eggplants for the evening meal but instead baked some brownies on the spur of the moment. She had baked brownies for dinner five nights in a row for herself and Madeline since they helped her feel better on her terrible days.

Madeline was watching TV with her mother when Harriet walked out on her suddenly. After the magazine came out, he was worried about Madeline and decided to see how she was doing.

They were having a conversation when Elizabeth arrived home early. She was watching the show's questions part. A woman inquired, "Is it true that my daughter was born illegitimate?" before she could turn it off.

Wakely got up to leave, but Elizabeth intercepted him. He didn't get to meet Calvin but admired him all the same, so he apologized for not introducing himself at the burial. He told Madeline that only moronic people gave a hoot about illegitimacy.

He added that he agreed with Elizabeth that "society" was "based on myth" (p. 343), but Elizabeth said that wasn't included in the magazine's print version.

Now he knew why he had come: Roth had left a letter for Elizabeth, Madeline had read it and brought it to Wakely. Madeline sobbed as she read the gruesome piece, for which she felt guilty due to her family's history.

A note attached to the letter explained that Roth had resigned and was lobbying for the publication of an honest story about her. The message included a fresh article that spoke well about her and other women in science.

Madeline was upset despite the positive story since she blamed herself (as Miss Frask had informed her) for Elizabeth's decision to become a TV chef rather than a chemist. Despite Madeline's claims to the contrary, Elizabeth is adamant that she is still a chemist.

## CHAPTER 39: DEAR SIRS

Madeline had met Miss Frask two days earlier at Wakely's office. Frask responded to Madeline's inquiry about her parents by saying they were a happy couple. This was the first time she had spoken without envy coloring her words.

Frask remembered how her jealous slander had led to Elizabeth's dismissal. It culminated in Elizabeth's return and subsequent confessions to Frask about his assaults and Elizabeth's failure to complete her studies, all contributing to their miserable employment situations in Hastings.

Madeline loathed the truth, but Frask tried to soften it by saying that Elizabeth was let go because she was expecting Madeline. Madeline took responsibility for her mother's loss of her scientific research position and was saddened. Although Madeline intended for Wakely to read Frask Roth's letter, he ended up reading it himself.

Frask was inspired by the letter praising Elizabeth's achievements in exposing the truth about Donatti's plagiarism and lying and Elizabeth's abuse at Hastings to the editors of Life magazine.

Elizabeth was unconcerned that Frask's letter would be published in the next issue with many other women's letters of support. She was down and out and had a hard time keeping going. She had always been able to shrug off setbacks, but now she wasn't sure if she could. She was irreparably damaged and demoralized by the publication. She told Harriet that no one cared about "women in science" (Garmus, 2022, p. 350), which completely shocked Harriet.

The events in Chapter 1 took place at Elizabeth's workplace.

As Harriet reflected on Elizabeth's statement that no one was interested in scientific women, she realized that perhaps she wasn't too responsible for Elizabeth's unhappiness after all.

## CHAPTER 40: NORMAL

Elizabeth told Wakely that she thought it was weird because she frequently thought about dying. An average person, he argued, may not exist, and he was the same. Even though he was a minister, he gave the impression that he didn't fully adhere to the Bible's teachings.

Elizabeth revealed that she had read their correspondence and was aware that Calvin had decided to take a job in Commons due to Wakely's glowing descriptions of the local climate. Wakely blamed himself for Calvin's death because of the decisions he had helped to shape. The survivors of Calvin's death are plagued by remorse and obligation.

He recalled the time at the end of Chapter 28 when he and Madeline had their little secret exchange. He informed her he didn't believe in God, and she murmured that Six-thirty knew about a thousand words, which he didn't think.

Elizabeth told Wakely that when she was a kid, she and her brother jumped into a quarry, and her brother rescued her. Before he passed away, she felt sorry that she hadn't been able to save him the way he had saved her. Despite Wakely's assertion that his actions were not tantamount to suicide, she disclosed that he, too, could not swim when he rescued her.

Wakely stated that people must learn to accept events beyond their control. He lauded her for not taking things at their value and for not getting the "unacceptable" (Garmus, 2022) (Calvin and her brother's death), but he also told her that part of being a scientist was bringing about change.

She said she wanted to go and go "out" like her brother, but Wakely thought she only wanted to come back "in" (Garmus, 2022, p. 356).

This suggests that she was depressed not because she intended to end her life but because she saw no way out. The excitement for life and science she felt before Calvin died was something she yearned to "get back in" to. She knew there was more for her to accomplish, more for her to prove, but she needed to figure out where to begin. Elizabeth seems to have understood Wakely's message, as evidenced by her behavior in the following chapter.

# CHAPTER 41: RECOMMIT

When Elizabeth unexpectedly visited Walter one night, she found the two of them in bed together with Harriet. He said that they had been secretly dating Elizabeth without her knowledge. Elizabeth announced her departure from the program. Harriet and Walter comforted and held her while crying.

The next day, Elizabeth announced that this would be her last episode of Supper at Six. It was universally unbelievable.

Elizabeth stated that she was returning to the field of chemistry and was pleased with the progress she and her audience had made over the past two years. She then read a letter from the Chapter 29 protagonist, a woman who wished to become an open heart surgeon, declaring that she had finished her training and was doing well. Elizabeth cracked a smile, undoubtedly a first for her on the show.

After reading what Wakely had to say in the previous chapter, Elizabeth was inspired to write "CHEMISTRY CHANGE" (Garmus, 2022, p. 360) on her easel. She urged women everywhere to reject labels of race, gender, religion, and socioeconomic status and to remember that courage is the bedrock of progress.

Elizabeth praised Harriet for the guidance she'd received from her on their first meeting, which she said was the source of her final tagline, and for prompting her to reflect on her own goals and needs, which ultimately led to her choice to quit the program. Elizabeth's fire and determination were reignited.

At the end, she used a remark Walter made up on the spot to acknowledge the show's true nature as an introduction to chemistry disguised as a cooking demonstration.

The fact that Walter came up with her final sentence on the television demonstrates how much he has developed as a person. He has shifted his focus from trying to convince Elizabeth to share Phil's superficial vision to focusing squarely on the show's pedagogical potential.

## CHAPTER 42: PERSONNEL

After the show concluded, many people, including Elizabeth, assumed she would receive numerous job offers. The comments of Donatti and Meyers had permanently damaged Elizabeth's scientific credibility. The public only wanted her because she hosted Supper at Six.

Elizabeth declined Harriet's offer to return to the program. Before leaving, Harriet revealed that Elizabeth had received a call from the director of Personnel at Hastings, Miss Frask. This was likely related to Harriet's impending divorce from Mr. Sloane. Elizabeth thought Frask was joking with Harriet because he had been fired long ago.

When Elizabeth called back, she was shocked to learn that everything she had heard was real. The wealthy sponsor who had disappeared after reading Frask's letter to Life magazine had reappeared, and Frask, now director of the department from which she had been sacked, wanted Elizabeth to come in.

Harriet remembered all the times she told the priest about her husband's abuse, and how the priest always begged her to change for him. She had tried to take his advice by reading publications, but after getting to know Elizabeth, she realized she was fine the way she was. She decided to utilize Roth's rejected article as the beginning of a career in the magazine industry. At the end of Chapter 39, she came up with this theory.

The Hastings secretary recognized Elizabeth and asked if she would autograph her latest magazine. Perplexed, Elizabeth looked through the magazine issue in which Harriet had found Roth's piece.

Elizabeth was urged to meet the sponsor, Avery Parker and Wilson, at Calvin's laboratory. Elizabeth politely declined their offer to continue her research at Hastings.

Donatti entered the laboratory abruptly, greeting only Wilson and showing disdain for Avery, Frask, and Elizabeth. Wilson clarified that they were aware of his dishonesty and financial scamming. Donatti attempted to blame the impending legal action on Frask's letter, but Wilson outed himself as Donatti's attorney. Avery gave Donatti an official notice of termination and treated him with the same disdain he had shown Elizabeth all those years earlier.

His shock was compounded when he learned that Elizabeth would be replacing him as head of the Chemistry department. She was given the authority to decide whether he would remain or leave, and she used it to her advantage by telling him he wasn't intelligent enough to stay.

## CHAPTER 43: STILLBORN

Avery stated as she escorted Donatti out the door, that, unlike Elizabeth, she was not married.

Elizabeth had previously mentioned that she was aware their foundation was eager to donate to places of worship like orphanages. Wilson said that their founders' focus had shifted from religion to science largely due to her and Calvin.

Elizabeth recalled that the wealthy man described in Calvin's diary was identical to Wilson. She wanted to know if they had ever donated books to a boys' shelter in Iowa.

Elizabeth wanted to talk to Wilson, but Avery had requested him to go so she could speak to Elizabeth alone.

Elizabeth suspected that they had faked the job offer to access Calvin's possessions and that Wilson was the dreaded biological father of Calvin. Avery said that Wilson was only her lawyer and the foundation's "face" (Garmus, 2022, p. 374); she had no children with Wilson.

Since Avery was a woman and required her nonexistent husband's consent to inherit her foundation, she had appointed Wilson to assist her in this role.

Avery felt terrible as the misunderstanding grew, and Elizabeth accused them of wanting only Calvin's belongings.

Avery related a story about a girl who got pregnant at seventeen after falling in love. Her devout parents abandoned her in a facility for pregnant and unwed women, reminiscent of a prison. She was told she had to sign away her kid, and when she refused, she went into labor without anyone else. The doctor finally got tired of the commotion and gave her an anesthetic; when she woke up, she was told that her baby had died shortly after birth. After bribing a nurse at the facility, the woman learned ten years later that her baby was still alive and began searching for him.

It was Avery who gave birth to Calvin.

## CHAPTER 44: THE ACORN

After hearing the unexpected news, Elizabeth thought back on the letters she had received from Calvin's "mother," who never stopped writing. Avery told Elizabeth that she'd sent Wilson to the residence because she was just as leery of frauds as her son. Elizabeth deduced that the fake news of Calvin's death was spread to Wilson for financial gain.

Elizabeth said that she had lost her brother to suicide when Avery inquired if she had ever lost someone. Avery responded mournfully by saying that they had an understanding of what it was like to bear responsibility for the death of a close family member.

After paying for the bogus ceremony and then losing Calvin, Avery felt as though she had buried him twice. Like Elizabeth, she was an atheist, but unlike Elizabeth, she was an atheist because the church had taken her son and told her he was dead.

In recognition of the fact that his biological father was a rower, she presented the family with educational materials and instruction in the sport. This is how Calvin honed his rowing skills and eventually enrolled at Cambridge.

Avery found out the truth when Calvin was on a magazine cover, but she chose to let him find out when he was ready, so she started writing him letters explaining what had happened. She should not have been so patient in retrospect.

Wilson rigorously sponsored abiogenesis because of the reports that Calvin and Elizabeth were together at Hastings, and Avery loved the difficult position that put Donatti in.

Wilson had anticipated meeting Elizabeth in person, knowing full well that she was a woman, but Calvin's untimely demise derailed those plans. The misleading coverage of Calvin's death and Elizabeth's relationship with him led Avery to believe the two weren't particularly close.

Even though Avery attended the burial, he never got to meet Elizabeth because she left so fast. Her assumption was incorrect; Elizabeth yelled out that her love for him was undying. They comforted and hugged each other while crying.

## CHAPTER 45: SUPPER AT SIX

At 6:30, one could see the intense love and friendship between the two women. Avery told Elizabeth that she didn't know much about Calvin's background until she got a letter from Madeline. Madeline's revelations helped Avery figure out the whole truth: Madeline had been murdered by the bishop because of her defiance at the women's home, and the bishop had given Calvin her "death certificate."

Avery showed Elizabeth a photo of Calvin's biological father, who greatly resembled the boy. The birth of Calvin came too late; he died of TB. While riding his bike, he accidentally ran over Avery; he later gave her a brooch that she still uses.

Elizabeth assured Avery she would share more details about Calvin in the future, even though their initial encounter was hardly a case of "love at first sight." Elizabeth remarked that she, and not Wilson, was the acorn on Madeline's family tree, making her feel like she was part of the family.

Wilson cut in because he and Avery needed to rush off to take care of some business before leaving the next day.

To extend Avery's visit, Elizabeth invited her and Wilson over for "supper at six" (Garmus, 2022, p. 386) so that Avery might meet Walter, Harriet, Elizabeth, Madeline, Dr. Mason, and Wakely. Just before she departed, Avery accepted with all her heart.

At the end of the book, Six-thirty tells the readers that he realized Avery was Calvin's mother at 2:42 p.m. (he'll refer to her as Avery from here on out) and picks up an empty notebook so that Elizabeth can continue her studies in abiogenesis.

## DEAR READER

Thank you for reading this entire book, which I know you could have easily skipped through, and for purchasing a legitimate copy to show your support for my efforts as an author.

Please consider leaving a review or rating on Amazon if you found the content helpful; I would appreciate it, and so would other readers. It's also the most efficient method of helping out underdog artists like me.

Post your thoughts here! >>


Much obliged,

Printed in the USA
CPSIA information can be obtained
at www.ICGtesting.com
LVHW020204271023
762248LV00048B/1070